Miracle

The Master Class Series

Miracle

The Ideas of Neville Goddard

A MASTER CLASS COURSE WITH

Mitch Horowitz

MEDIA

Published 2019 by Gildan Media LLC
aka G&D Media
www.GandDmedia.com

FIRST EDITION 2019

Front Cover design by David Rheinhardt of Pyrographx

Interior design by Meghan Day Healey of Story Horse, LLC

Library of Congress Cataloging-in-Publication Data is available upon request

ISBN: 978-1-7225-0017-7

10   9   8   7   6   5   4   3   2   1

Contents

Introduction

Welcome to the Master Class Series. Each of these courses instructs you, in ten simple, straightforward lessons, how to benefit from the causative powers of your mind.

The lessons are designed so that you may experience one each day, all of them at once, or in whatever configuration you want. Do the exercises in your own time and at your own pace—but it is crucial that you *do them*. This series supplies hands-on philosophy. At the end of each course, you'll find a short quiz to reinforce your knowledge.

The Master Class Series is designed to provide you with a new estimate of yourself, and of your highest possibilities.

Lesson
ONE

Extremist Self-Responsibility

What is a good way to live? This question has occupied the human mind since man's earliest attempts at self-expression.

When seeking the good life, we are often caught in a sense of denial. We make a nod—and rightly so—to Golden Rule ethics; but we omit the indelible fact that most of us are also searching for some semblance of personal power, for the ability to enact and see through our plans in the world.

Where can this power be found? Does it even exist? Imagine for a moment that your emotionalized thoughts and mental images literally create everything in your world. How would that change your life? Would you be willing to test such a proposition?

That was the challenge brought to modern life by Neville Goddard, a twentieth-century metaphysical philosopher and lecturer who issued the dramatic claim that the human imagination is God. Neville wrote under his first name, which reflects how I'll refer to him in this course.

The mystic and teacher argued, with elegance and congruity, that any time you encounter the term God, Yahweh, or Christ in the Old or New Testaments, you are actually encountering an allegorical reference to *your own* thoughts and emotive states, which literally outpicture the reality around you.

Each of us, Neville taught, is literally the Creator clothed in human flesh, slumbering to his own divinity. We live, he said, within an infinite network of coexistent realities, from which we select (rather than create) experiences by the nature of our emotionalized thoughts and expectations. In that sense, the words that you are now encountering are your own words—they are rooted in you, as you are ultimately rooted in God. The other men and women you see about you are also branches of the Creator: we each crisscross throughout one another's universe of formative thought systems, until we experience the ultimate realization—the crucifixion on the cross of awareness—that awakens us to our Providential nature.

If this all seems rather breathless, let's step back for a moment. Neville was not dogmatic on any count. He defended his ideas with an elegant simplicity, and challenged the listener simply: try it. "I hope you will be bold enough to test me," he offered. Have we lost our taste for individual experimentation?

As we will explore later in this course, some of Neville's ideas are also surprisingly congruent with concepts in quantum physics. His outlook is probably the closest mystical analog to quantum theory.

Now, I have also written in many books and articles that I do not believe we live under one overarching mental super law. We live under many laws and forces, of which the law of mental creativity is one crucial aspect—as are, in my view, accident, physicality, and death.

That is my outlook, which I further explore later in this course. That said, there is so much that we do not know, mentally, physically, and existentially, and I believe that every dedicated seeker is a kind of existential scientist in his or her own right. We must test the outer reaches of our ideas. That is the simple aim Neville urged on us, and to which this short course is dedicated.

Lesson
TWO

Who Was Neville?

The philosophy called New Thought is a mystical and psychological teaching that arose in the wake of New England Transcendentalism in the late-nineteenth century. It promulgates one core principle: *thoughts are causative.* This outlook is, in varying forms, at the heart of American spirituality, ranging from New Age mysticism to self-help movements like Alcoholics Anonymous to evangelical mega-ministries.

Perhaps the most intriguing and substantive teacher of New Thought in the years following World War II was the figure at the heart of this course: a Barbados-born dancer and stage actor, who cultivated a mysterious biography, and went by the singular name, Neville.

Born in 1905 to an English family in the West Indies, Neville Lancelot Goddard arrived in New York City in the early 1920s, at age seventeen, to study theater. His ambition for the stage faded as he came in contact with various mystical and occult philosophies.

By the early 1930s, Neville embarked on a new and unforeseen career as a lecturer and writer of mind-power metaphysics. In lectures, Neville often referred to an enigmatic, turbaned black man named Abdullah who he said tutored him in Scripture, number mysticism, Kabbalah, and Hebrew.

Whatever the source of Neville's education, his outlook reflected not only the most occultic edge of New Thought, but also the philosophy's most intellectually stimulating expression. Neville saw each individual as a potential God. The aware person could select from among a universe of infinite realities, all brought into existence by a mixture of one's mind's-eye imagery and emotive states. *That which we think, feel, and see to be true*, Neville taught, *literally is true*. In Neville's viewpoint, our active imagination—that is, our thoughts and corresponding feelings—creates reality.

In lectures and books, Neville described how his West Indian family prospered at the helm of a food service and catering business—and these claims do conform to public records. Claims that others made about him, by contrast, were sometimes fanciful. In 1955, a Hollywood gossip columnist called Neville "enormously wealthy," his family possessing "a whole island in the West Indies." That is a gross exaggeration. Despite the Goddard family's eventual business success, it began as a modest, scrappy clan, and Neville's material existence as a young man was precarious, a fact he never disguised.

While he landed roles on Broadway and toured as part of a ballroom dancing duo, the young Neville lived hand-to-mouth in New York, working for a time as an elevator operator and shipping clerk. In pursuit of spiritual awareness, the performer experimented with ascetic living, eschewing meat, dairy, tobacco, and alcohol. At one point, his weight dropped from 176 to 135 pounds.

By 1930, Neville felt physically unwell, and no closer to peering into life's mysteries. But he experienced a dramatic turnaround, he said, upon meeting a mysterious spiritual mentor named Abdullah. In Neville's recollection, his first meeting with Abdullah had an air of kismet:

When I first met my friend Abdullah back in 1931 I entered a room where he was speaking and when the speech was ended he came over, extended his hand and said: 'Neville, you are six months late.' I had never seen the man before, so I said: 'I am six months late? How do

*you know me?' and he replied: 'The brothers
told me that you were coming and you are six
months late.'*

Writing about Neville in the 1940s, the occult
philosopher Israel Regardie called Abdullah
an "eccentric Ethiopian rabbi." The descrip-
tion stuck, and Neville's apprenticeship under
an "African rabbi" became part of his mythos.

Following this fateful encounter, Neville
said that he and Abdullah spent five years to-
gether studying Hebrew, Scripture, number
symbolism, and mystical religions—planting
the seeds of Neville's philosophy of mental creativity.

Neville recalled first grasping the potential
of creative thought while he was living in a
rented room on Manhattan's Upper West Side
in the winter of 1933. The young man was de-
pressed: his theatrical career had stalled, and
he was broke. "After twelve years in America,
I was a failure in my own eyes," he said. "I
was in the theater and made money one year
and spent it the next month." The 28-year-old
ached to spend Christmas with his family in
Barbados, but he couldn't afford to travel.

"Live as though you are there," Abdullah
told him, "and that you shall be." Wandering
the streets of New York City, Neville adopted
the *feeling state* that he was really and truly at

home on his native island. "Abdullah taught me the importance of remaining faithful to an idea and not compromising," he remembered. On a December morning, before the last ship that year was to depart for Barbados, Neville received a letter from a long out-of-touch brother: tucked inside were $50 and an ocean-liner reservation.

The episode sealed Neville's belief in the powers of the mind, which he would express in thousands of lectures and more than ten books until his death in West Hollywood in 1972. Neville wanted to be remembered less for his persona, however, than for his method of mental creativity, to which we now turn.

Lesson
THREE

The Method

The method behind Neville's philosophy is reducible to a three-part formula. This formula is simple, but do not approach it lightly. It requires persistence. For the following three lessons, we will explore each of the three steps involved in Neville's method. We now approach the first step, which begins with clarifying your wants.

Step 1. Every creative act begins with a passionate desire.

"You must know what you want before you can ask for it," Neville wrote in 1945. Do not be fooled by how easy that sounds. We walk around all day with scattershot desires, thinking: I want this and that; I want money; I want sex and romance; I want this person to pay attention to me; I want this achievement; and so

on. Yet much of the time, we have only super-
ficial understandings of our desires. We're dis-
honest about what we truly want, because we
often don't want to acknowledge, in our inner-
most hearts, what we really wish for.

We live in a society that is, on the surface,
filled with personal license and freedom; but
we don't like admitting to ourselves things that
we feel are unfitting of a given image we've
cultivated—a self-image designed to appeal to
others, but that may no longer fit us. We also
confuse *means* with *desires*, sometimes saying
we want a certain job, for example, when what
we really want is security.

When Neville talks about desire, he's not
speaking superficially. He really wants you
to get down into the guts of matters, where
you might discover a desire for something
that makes you uncomfortable, like personal
power. There are ways we don't like to see ourselves. But Neville maintains that desire is God
speaking to us. And God *is* us. To walk away
from a deep personal yearning is to walk away
from God within yourself.

In essence, we all want the same thing: to
fulfill our essential inner ideals, to exercise,
exhibit, and exert ourselves in the natural di-
rection toward which we feel drawn. And we
want to be seen and understood.

I was once in spiritual group where a woman described in a meeting how she had made an ice sculpture outside of her home on a bright winter day. Some friends came to visit in the afternoon, and she was anxious that they see her sculpture before it melted in the sun. She was embarrassed to direct her friends' attention to it, yet at the same time she was eager for her work to be seen. The woman recounted this as a kind of a confession, expressed with remorse over her presumed egotism. I honor the self-disclosure with which she told her story—yet I feel strongly that she had nothing to feel ashamed of, and nothing to confess. She created something beautiful. She had the ability to do so. Why shouldn't she want her friends to see it—why hide her light under a bushel? Her work made the world more beautiful before it was taken by the afternoon sun, and her act spoke of her to the world; which is to say it spoke of all human creativity.

Self-expression is to be honored. Creative acts are to be seen. Your clarified desire is the language of holiness; it is the urge toward creation. "And God saw that it was good." Be exquisitely clear, passionate, and forthright about your goals.

This prepares us for the second step, which begins the process of actualization.

Lesson
FOUR

Impregnating the Mind

We now move to:

Step 2. Your imagination is fertilized in a state of physical immobility.

This is where we start to *enact* our desires. Creativity begins when we purposefully enter a state of physical immobility. Choose a time of day when you would like to meditate. The time of day Neville chose was 3 p.m. He'd eat lunch, get tired, and willingly enter a drowsy state, usually in an easy chair; though a sofa, bed, or yoga mat would work just as well.

Now, this is very important, because we often think of meditation as a state of keen awareness or mindfulness. We don't think of meditation as drowsiness. People use these terms in different ways. Neville believed that we heighten our apparatus of mental creativity when we enter the "in between" state of consciousness called hypnagogia. The hypnagogic state is the stage between wakefulness and sleep. You're in it at night just as you're drifting off; you're in it in the morning just as you're coming to. At such times, our minds are deeply sensitive and impressionable.

People who suffer from depression or grief often describe the early morning hours as the most difficult time of day. The reason, I'm convinced, is that our rational defenses are down. We are conscious and have sensory awareness; but we are also in a deeply suggestible, impressionable state, in which emotions are powerfully felt. We lack a sense of proportionality. I can attest from experience that if you are trying to solve a personal problem, never attempt it while laying bed at 5 a.m. Do not. Get up and meditate, read, watch television, or do whatever you must, but keep in mind that your logical apparatus is at its ebb, and the gremlins of the unconscious are liable to run amuck.

When your analytic mind is at a low point and your emotions are churning, it is a very difficult time to confront problems, or attempt acts of perspective. But it is also, and for some of the same reasons, *a propitious time to visu-*

alize your desires. With your rational barriers down, your mind, if properly harnessed, can take you in remarkable directions. As I've written elsewhere, psychical researchers have made the extraordinary finding, studied under strict conditions, that when subjects are induced into a state of relaxed hypnagogia, usually through comfortable sensory deprivation, such as sitting with eyeshades and headphones in an isolation chamber, the mind is found to possess heightened abilities of extra-physical communication.

Neville said to enter a state of physical immobility of this sort. You may find it easiest to do just before you go to sleep at night. He didn't say to do it in the morning, but I think we can extrapolate that's a viable time, too. You can do it during a time that you set aside for meditating, as long as you're comfortable and undisturbed, and can uninhibitedly enter a very relaxed physical state. If you have difficulty relaxing, as many people do, allow the body to take over naturally by entering and becoming aware of this state before drifting off at night.

You will, however, need to do the next step—step three—*before* falling asleep, because it requires a measure of conscious control over your thoughts.

Lesson
FIVE

Hatching the Results

We now reach our third and final step in creation, which is:

Step 3. Form a vivid, simple mental scene of your desire fulfilled.

A woman at one of Neville's Los Angeles lectures told him that she yearned to be married—what should she do? He told her to enact the feeling of a ring on her finger. Just that. Mentally assume the feeling of a ring on your finger, in a very simple, natural way. Feel its weight, the density of the band, and maybe feel yourself spinning it around on your finger. Don't do anything physically, just feel it.

What you do want? Maybe you want something from another individual. Enact a scene that implies its fulfillment. Maybe just a handshake—something that communicates that you've received what you wanted, that it's done. *Do not see yourself doing this action as if you're watching it on a screen. Rather, you must feel yourself in the action, and see it from the perspective of actually performing it. You're not watching, you're performing.* If I want to imagine myself climbing a ladder, Neville said, I do not see myself climbing a ladder—*I climb!*

Make your mental scene very basic; it keeps the mind from wandering. Identify one clear physical action that communicates the attainment of your goal, *and then think and feel from that end.* Always think from the end of the goal fulfilled.

Neville told listeners that when you open your eyes, you'll be back here, in the ordinary world, which you might not want to be in; but if you persist in this practice, your assumption will eventually harden into fact. If you want to be in Paris and you open your eyes and you're still in Queens, you may be disappointed. But keep doing it. An extraordinary event, he taught, will unfold to secure what you have pictured.

One point must be clarified—and this point must be stated more clearly throughout New Thought culture in general. Neville noted that the visual state must also be accompanied by an emotive state. The positive-thinking movement often errs in equating thoughts with emotions. They are entirely different. I have a physical existence, I have an intellectual existence, and I have an emotional existence. The reason we feel so torn apart is because these things are all going their own way. I say that I'm not going to eat something—well, the body wants to eat it, and next thing it's my mouth. I resolve to be calm—but the emotions are furious, and I experience an outburst. I determine that I'm going to think, to use my intellect—but my passions are running off doing something else.

When you enact your mental picture of fulfillment, you must experience the emotions that you would feel in your state of achievement. This method may come naturally to some people, including those who are actors. Neville himself was an actor and performer. Anyone who has studied Method Acting learns to use an inner monologue to enter an emotional state. That's a useful exercise. Read Constantin Stanislavsky's *An Actor Prepares*. You must get your emotions into play. Let's say you want a promotion at work. You might picture your boss shaking your hand and saying "congratulations, congratulations." You have to *feel* the emotions that would naturally be yours in that state. "Feeling is the secret," Neville wrote.

It is the mental-emotional state, and not physical effort, that creates, he taught. Some people ask whether this is a formula for passivity. I am friendly with a successful manufacturing executive in the Midwest. He is an avid student of Neville's ideas. He asked me a question one day: He feels confident in picturing an outcome. But his board of directors, he explained, demands details—they want to know: how will it get done? In following Neville's teachings, he feels that he's already doing all that is needed. And for years it has worked. But he must answer to people who aren't going to accept a metaphysical formula as a business plan. What should he do?

My response to him was to plan and act as the board requires—and continue to mentally create as before, remaining true to his conviction that that's where the real power resides. We live in a world of Caesar, and must abide by material demands. My friend will lose the confidence of his board if he fails to act. We are called upon to perform in both worlds: the seen and the unseen. If Neville wanted to take a train somewhere, he didn't just sit in his room—he went out and purchased a ticket. We are surrounded by people living in outer life. Play the role that outer life requires. "Render unto Caesar." But remember the underground spring from which all creation arises.

There is one further aspect to the act of mental actualization: creative silence. Do not blurt out what you're attempting, or act hastily to move things along. Ralph Waldo Emerson captured this principle in a passage from his journals of January 15, 1857:

> *This good which invites me now is visible & specific. I will at least embrace it this time by way of experiment, & if it is wrong certainly God can in some manner signify his will in future. Moreover I will guard against evil consequences resulting to others by the vigilance with which I conceal it.*

In other words, we risk no harm to ourselves and others in our acts of mental intention, provided *we avoid rash outer action.* For example, let's say you harbor romantic feelings toward someone. To speak of it could cause embarrassment, rejection, or ruinous consequences. Do not speak. Allow your mind to act; if you are wrong (as you may be) you will eventually know by perception. And if you are correct, events will unfold harmoniously, as good events always do and must from God—your mind—who speaks in the Beatitudes of gentleness, love of neighbor, and generosity.

So, to recap the formula: *First,* clarify a sincere and deeply felt desire. *Second,* enter a state of relaxed immobility, bordering on sleep. *Third*, enact a mental scene that contains the assumption and feeling of your wish fulfilled. Run the little drama over and over in your mind until you experience a sense of fulfillment. Then resume your life. Evidence of your achievement will unfold at the right moment in your outer experience.

Lesson
SIX

Quantum Physics and the Mind, Part I

In order to consider what may be the most important aspect of Neville's legacy, we must take a brief journey away from his career before returning to it. Our purpose in this lesson is to look at the importance of quantum theory for metaphysical thinkers, and how Neville's outlook relates to it.

If you're taking this course, you're probably aware that a growing wave of New Age books and documentaries use quantum theory to "prove" the idea that *thoughts are causative*. Many quantum physicists protest that crystal gazers have mangled the implications of these experiments, in which measurements of subatomic particles are affected by the presence or decisions of an observer.

The truth is: quantum physics *does* raise extraordinary questions about the nature of the mind. More than eighty years of laboratory experiments demonstrate that atomic-scale particles appear in a given place only when a measurement is made. Astonishing as it sounds—and physicists themselves have debated the data for generations—quantum theory holds that *no measurement means no precise and localized object,* on the atomic level.

Put differently, a subatomic particle literally occupies an infinite number of places (a state called "superposition") until observation manifests it in one place. In quantum mechanics, a decision to look or not look actually determines what will appear where. In this sense, an observer's consciousness determines objective reality in the subatomic field.

Some physicists would dispute that characterization. Critics sometimes argue that certain particles are too small to measure; hence any attempt at measurement inevitably affects what is seen. But there exists a whole class of "interaction-free measurement" quantum experiments that don't involve detectors at all. Such experiments have repeatedly shown that a subatomic object literally exists in more than one place at once until a measurement determines its final resting spot.

How is this actually provable? In the parlance of quantum physics, an atomic-scale particle is said to exist in a wave-state, which means that the location of the particle in space-time is known only probabilistically; it has no properties in this state, just potentialities. When particles or waves—typically in the form of a beam of photons or electrons—are directed or aimed at a target system, such as a double-slit, scientists have found that their pattern or path will actually change, or "collapse," depending upon the presence or measurement choices of an observer. Hence, a wave pattern will shift into a particle pattern. Contrary to all reason, quantum theory holds that opposing outcomes simultaneously exist.

The situation gets even stranger—and leads closer to Neville's way of thought—when dealing with the famous thought experiment known as "Schrodinger's cat," to which we turn in our next lesson.

Lesson
SEVEN

Quantum Physics and the Mind, Part II

The twentieth-century physicist Erwin Schro-dinger was frustrated with the evident absur-dity of quantum theory, which showed objects simultaneously appearing in more than one place at a time. Such an outlook, he felt, vio-lated all commonly observed physical laws. In 1935, Schrodinger sought to highlight this predicament through a purposely absurdist thought experiment, which he intended to force quantum physicists to follow their data to its ultimate ends.

Schrodinger reasoned that quantum data dictates that a sentient being, such as a cat, can be simultaneously alive and dead. A variant of the "Schrodinger's cat" experiment could be put this way: Let's say a cat is placed into one of a pair of boxes. Along with the cat is what Schrodinger called a "diabolical device." The device, if exposed to an atom, releases a deadly poison. An observer then fires an atom at the boxes. The observer subsequently uses some form of measurement to check on which box the atom is in: the empty one, or the one with the cat and the poisoning device. When the observer goes to check, the wave function of the atom—i.e., the state in which it exists in both boxes—collapses into a particle function—i.e., the state in which it is localized to one box. Once the observer takes his measurement, convention says that the cat will be discovered to be dead or alive. But Schrodinger reasoned that quantum physics describes an outcome in which the cat is *both* dead and alive. This is because the atom, in its wave function, was, at one time, in either box, and either outcome is real.

To take it even further, a cohort of quantum physicists in the 1950s theorized that if an observer waited some significant length of time, say, eight hours, before checking on the dead-alive cat, he would discover one cat that was dead for eight hours and another that was alive for eight hours (and is now hungry). In this line of reasoning, conscious observation effectively manifested the localized atom, the dead cat, the living cat—and *also manifested the past*, i.e., created a history for both a dead cat and a living one. Both outcomes are true.

Absurd? Impossible? Yes to that, say quantum physicists—but decades of quantum experiments make this model—in which a creature can be dead/alive—into an impossible reality: an unbelievable yet entirely tenable, even necessary, state of nature. Only future experiments will determine the broader implications of sub-atomic phenomena in the mechanical world in which we live.

For now, however, decades of quantum data make it defensible to conclude that observation done on the subatomic scale: (1) shapes the nature of outcomes, (2) determines the presence or absence of a localized object, and (3) possibly devises multiple pasts and presents. This last point is sometimes called the "many-worlds interpretation," in the words of physicist Hugh Everett. This theory of "many worlds" raises the prospect of an infinite number of realities and states of being, each depending upon our choices.

In effect, this is exactly what Neville describes from a metaphysical perspective. In our next lesson, we explore how Neville provides the closest New Thought analog to quantum theory.

Lesson
EIGHT

Explorer of the Infinite

In our previous lesson, I mentioned the theories of quantum physicist Hugh Everett. Everett theorized the existence of multiple worlds and outcomes based on the choices and perspective of the observer. His way of thought runs closely parallel to Neville's.

Neville made this observation in 1948: "Scientists will one day explain why there is a serial universe. But in practice, how you use this serial universe to change the future is more important."

Recall that Neville taught that everything we see and experience is the product of what happens in our own individual dream of reality. Through a combination of emotional conviction and mental images, Neville said, each person imagines his world into being—all people and events are rooted in us, as we are ultimately rooted in the highest source of creation, or God. When a person awakens to his true self, Neville argued, he will, in fact, discover himself to be a slumbering branch of the Creator clothed in human form, and at the helm of infinite possibilities.

Neville's formula is simplicity itself. To reiterate: *First*, clarify you desire. *Second*, assume a state of physical immobility, a deeply relaxed state similar to what you experience just before drifting to sleep. *Third*, enact in your mind a small, satisfying drama that implies the wish fulfilled, such as someone congratulating you or your holding an award. Repeat this internal drama over and over, as long as it is vivid and emotionally charged.

"Take my challenge and put my words to the test," Neville told listeners in 1949. "If the law does not work, its knowledge will not comfort you. And if it is not true, you must discard it . . . I hope you will be bold enough to test me."

Now, most quantum physicists wouldn't be caught dead/alive as Schrodinger's cat reading an occult philosopher like Neville. Indeed, many physicists reject the notion of interpreting the larger implications of quantum data at all. "Shut up and calculate!" is the battle cry popularized by physicist N. David Mermin.

The role of physics, critics insist, is to *measure things*—not, in Einstein's phrase, to lift "the veil that shrouds the Old One." Others adopt the opposite position: If physics isn't for explaining reality, then what *is* it for?

The latter principle may carry the day. A new generation of physicists and theorists, raised in the sixties and seventies—and open to questions of consciousness—is gaining prominence. Medical researcher Robert Lanza, M.D., of the Institute for Regenerative Medicine at Wake Forest University, uses quantum theory to argue that death itself is ultimately a mental phenomenon: we "die" only insofar as the mind perceives demise. Psychiatrist Jeffrey M. Schwartz of UCLA links quantum physics with his research into how thoughts alter brain biology, concluding that "directed, willed mental activity . . . generates a *physical* force."

Quantum physics brings us to a threshold of inquiry that may redefine what it means to be human in the twenty-first century, as much as the theory of evolution did in the Victorian age. Seen in this light, Neville, an explorer of the infinite, may come to be regarded as the most foresightful spiritual philosopher of our time.

Lesson
NINE

Do We Live In a Mental Universe?

Neville argues, with elegance and suppleness, that we live under one ultimate law of mentation. Is that true? Nothing in his philosophy, or any other, should be taken at face value. When testing a religious or ethical idea we possess only the empiricism of inner experience. Each individual must verify religious or ethical claims for himself. The measures of verification appear in the effects of an idea on one's conduct and relationships, and in its results across daily life.

It is insufficient, and can even be misleading, to sit in a chair nodding my head in agreement as I read a given principle. Rather, I must know what that applied principle does for me at 3 p.m. on Thursday.

When searching people hear of Neville's claims, it is entirely natural for them to ask about the existence of personal agonies and tragedies—including those that strike people who evince deep love and zest for life. They wonder about large-scale disasters, such as earthquakes in Haiti and Mexico, and hurricanes in the Philippines and Puerto Rico, which leave behind disease, hunger, maimed victims, and mass fatalities—all without any obvious sense of justice.

These are not weak-minded or conventional questions—they are urgent ones. But please notice how I began this passage—by referring to the questions of "searching people." When these questions are asked by truly *seeking* individuals, they are valuable because they arise from a sincere and authentic inquiry. When such dilemmas are raised as rhetorical propositions by the cynic, or the person who has no ethical or religious search, and for whom the spiritual question evokes only eye-rolling, they are of no value: they are simply devices to reinforce preexisting beliefs that our lives are solely material, and that our minds are no more than epiphenomena of brain matter.

So, it is to the true seeker, and not the cynic, that I describe my own struggle with the question of whether we live under one ultimate law of mental creativity. Based on my personal search up to this point, I believe we live under many laws and forces, including accident, natural events, and physical limitations. Mortality alone tells us that. And yet . . . I am unprepared to say Neville was wrong. In fact, due to a combination of personal experience, and compelling developments in quantum theory, I believe he may very likely be right that consciousness—or awareness, as I prefer it—is the ultimate arbiter of reality.

However—and this is key to what I am arguing—other factors may interrupt or mitigate our experience of the mind's primacy. We may be unable, most of the time, to experience the fact of consciousness-based reality on the physical scale. Now, a law, in order to be a law, must be consistent. So, if I concede that the mind may be the ultimate arbiter of reality, why do events seem to diverge from, or contradict, our emotionalized thoughts and mental images? A hint may come from considering the law of gravity. Gravitation is consistent. But you are going to experience its effects much differently on the moon, where you can jump ten feet in the air, than, say, on the planet Jupiter, where gravity's force would crush you. The law is at always work. But gravity is affected by mass. Its absence, such as in space, where there is no mass, does not indicate suspension of the ever-operative law, but rather reflects an alteration of circumstance affecting how it is experienced. The same phenomenon may occur with our minds, which his why we experience the law of mentation with brilliant clarity at some points, and as a rollercoaster of inconsistent results at others. This apparent schism arises neither from misperception, nor failure of application. You can train your intellect all you like, but I propose that other factors, of which we are either unaware or only fleetingly aware, interfere with the ultimate experience and out-workings of mental causation on our plane of existence. These other factors may include physical forces that operate within their own cosmic framework.

This is why I insist that Neville did not leave us with a doctrine, but with articles of experimentation. Again, everything that I propose in these lessons must be tested in the laboratory of personal experience. Inner empiricism is our one tool on the spiritual path. For that reason, I dislike hearing certain people within the New Age or New Thought culture speak confidently about what was going on, from a metaphysical perspective, in 9/11 or the Holocaust, or in natural calamities, when they haven't personally gone through such things. Let those who *have* gone through them teach us about them. Of that which we haven't experienced, we must remain silent. Certainty is biography, or it is nothing. Hence, self-experiment is imperative; it is our one means of inner knowing.

In medical literature, I am inspired by the example of Australian psychiatrist Ainslee Meares, who died in 1986. In the last two decades of his life, Meares conducted intensive studies of terminal caner patients who had experienced spontaneous remission. About 20 such cases are reported in world medical literature each year. Meares documented a small number of cases in which intensive meditation seemed to correlate with spontaneous remission—but he was exquisitely measured and careful on the question. In the British medical journal *The Lancet* of November 7, 1981, Meares wrote:

> *In medicine we no longer expect to find a single cause for a disease; rather we expect to find a multiplicity of factors, organic and psychological. It is not suggested that psychological reactions, either psychosomatic or hysterical, are a direct cause of cancer. But it seems likely that reactions resembling those of psychosomatic illness and conversion hysteria operate as causes of cancer, more so in some cases than in others, and that they operate in connection with the know chemical, viral, and radiational causes of the disease.*

A theory of metaphysics is no less elegant for allowing multiple factors, as Meares did, rather than one overarching cause. Never feel bound by the contention that all of life is subject to a single law.

It should also be noted that Neville's vision was about more than a mental law of cause-and-effect. We now turn, in our closing lesson, to the teacher's ultimate view of life.

Lesson
TEN

Resurrection: Neville's Ultimate Vision

Of the more than ten books that Neville wrote, *Resurrection*, published in 1966, is named by many of his admirers as their personal favorite. The anthology was Neville's last published book, and it provides the full scope of his mystical and psychological insight. The book culminates in a complete spiritual system, in which Neville illuminates his vision of life and human purpose—which is realization of oneself as the Divine.

Four of the five works collected in *Resurrection* are actually deeply practical pamphlets and short studies that Neville published in the 1940s, when he came into his voice as a mystic and teacher. But he named the collection for its closing work, *Resurrection*, which he wrote just six years before his death. It is in *Resurrection* that Neville presents his ideas in their full bloom of maturity.

In understanding Neville's life and work, it is important to realize that his thought significantly broadened after 1959, a year that opened him to a series of mystical awakenings. This cycle of revelation had actually begun years earlier, he does not pinpoint exactly when, when he reported being "taken in spirit into a Divine Society," and then returned to earth "tormented by my limitations of understanding." These limitations began to lift in July 1959 when the teacher underwent a mystical rebirth, or resurrection, from within the womb of his own skull.

Following that experience by five months, in December 1959, Neville encountered the biblical figure of David who addressed him lovingly as "Father," confirming his Oneness with God. Four months thereafter, in April 1960, Neville experienced the opening of his body by a bolt of lightning to reveal a Divine luminous fluid within, representing the living water of God.

Neville called this cycle of rebirth "the Promise"—a process of self-realization that awaits all men and women as they come to understand, fully and experientially, that they are Christ clothed in the flesh.

In the essay *Resurrection*, Neville adds one further stage to his realization. He describes the fulfillment of Christ's three-and-a-half year ministry on earth with the Holy Spirit descending upon man in the form of a dove, bringing complete and final union with God. According to my calculations, Neville may have experienced this fourth stage in January 1963, but his telling leaves it unclear.

None of these experiences, of course, can be fully understood using our ordinary points of reference: They are neither strictly physical nor strictly belonging to some ethereal or spirit realm; they are, in Neville's teaching, revelations of a Higher Reality, which comes into focus with the unfolding of our Divine nature.

Neville first wrote about his mystical rebirth in his 1961 book, *The Law and the Promise*. But the details in *Resurrection* help us better understand the phenomena involved. In *Resurrection,* Neville provides a series of Biblical citations, which sync his experiences to Scripture while illuminating and giving further meaning to the events themselves. In a sense, *The Law and the Promise* tells us what occurred; in *Resurrection* we learn why it occurred.

Anyone who approaches *Resurection* for practical ideas, and finds all of this mysticism a bit heady, need not worry. Neville's culminating essay is preceded by four exquisitely practical, useful lessons in deploying the power of your imagination. *Resurrection* provides the full arc of Neville's teaching. This is why it is often considered his crowning expression.

Recent to this writing, I narrated an audio edition of *Resurrection,* in which I provide Neville's original words as he set them down. Over the years, publishers, perhaps seeking to bring colloquial familiarity to the text, have made small and, in my view, unnecessary alterations to Neville's work, sometimes omitting or changing a word or reference that was presumably considered opaque. I believe in preserving Neville's words exactly as he wrote them when he took inspiration from Isaiah 30:8: "And now go write it before them on a tablet, and inscribe it in a book, that it may be for the time to come as a witness forever."

Neville's teaching is not only a practical way of life but, ultimately, as a complete vision of life. It delivers what he called a "framework of faith, a faith leading to the fulfillment of God's promise."

My wish is that all of Neville's ideas open you to your highest possibilities.

We now turn to a 10-question quiz to reinforce your knowledge of this course. Each question has four choices, and one correct answer.

Quiz

1. To begin Neville's system, you must first:
   a) Meditate.
   b) Define a sincere goal.
   c) Go to sleep.
   d) Read *Resurrection*.

The correct answer is: b) Define a sincere goal.

2. Neville's method of visualizing requires:
   a) Seeing yourself as if on a movie screen.
   b) Saying an affirmation.
   c) Drawing a picture.
   d) Imagining yourself in the act.

The correct answer is: d) Imagining yourself in the act.

3. Neville's family was:
   a) Enormously wealthy.
   b) Estranged from him.
   c) Of modest means and grew successful.
   d) Atheists.

The correct answer is: c) Of modest means and grew successful.

4. Neville told listeners, "I hope you will be bold enough to . . ."
   a) "Ignore me."
   b) "Test me."
   c) "Read my books."
   d) "Share my ideas."

The correct answer is: b) "Test me."

5. The "many worlds" theory in quantum physics holds that:
   a) Truth is relative.
   b) Physicists often disagree.
   c) Space is vast.
   d) Infinite realities are possible.

The correct answer is: d) Infinite realities are possible.

6. Medical researcher Ainslie Meares
   believed that cancer arose from:
   a) Our minds.
   b) Myriad conditions.
   c) Heredity.
   d) Environmental factors.

The correct answer is: b) Myriad conditions.

7. Hypnagogia is the state:
   a) In between wakefulness and sleeping.
   b) Of dreaming.
   c) Of anxiety.
   d) Of REM sleep.

*The correct answer is: a) In between wakeful-
ness and sleeping.*

8. In quantum physics "superposition"
   means that a particle:
   a) Is in space.
   b) Cannot be detected.
   c) Occupies an infinite number of places.
   d) Binds with other particles.

*The correct answer is: c) Occupies an infinite
number of places.*

9. The thought experiment called
   "Schrodinger's cat" demonstrates:
      a) Simultaneous states of reality.
      b) How to split the atom.
      c) The weight of sub-atomic particles.
      d) The nature of felines.

The correct answer is: a) Simultaneous states of reality.

10. Neville's ultimate vision is:
      a) To get what you want.
      b) Union with God.
      c) Health and happiness.
      d) World peace.

The correct answer is: b) Union with God.

*   *   *

Thank you for taking this Master Class Course—and please check out the others in our Master Class Series. I hope this short program provides you with lessons and ideas that you will experiment with and benefit from over the course of your life.

About the Author

MITCH HOROWITZ is a writer and publisher with a lifelong interest in man's search for meaning. He is a PEN Award-winning historian and the author of books including *Occult America* and *One Simple Idea: How Positive Thinking Reshaped Modern Life.* Mitch has written on everything from the war on witches to the secret life of Ronald Reagan for *The New York Times, The Wall Street Journal, Salon,* and *Time. com. The Washington Post* says Mitch "treats esoteric ideas and movements with an even-handed intellectual studiousness that is too often lost in today's raised-voice discussions." Visit him at www.MitchHorowitz.com and @MitchHorowitz.